The Book
of
Inspirational
Short Sayings
&
Quotes

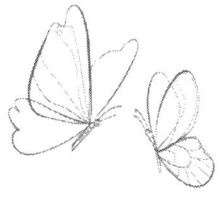

By Audrey J. Kornegay

Copyright © 2023 by Audrey J. Kornegay

All rights reserved. No part of this publication may be reproduced, stored or transmitted in any form or by any means, electronic, mechanical, photocopying, recording, scanning, or otherwise, without written permission from the publisher. It is illegal to copy this book, post it to a website, or distribute it by any other means without permission. First edition

Scripture quotations marked:
EVS – English Standard Version
KJV - King James Version
NIV - New International Version
NKJV - New King James Version
NLT - New Living Translation
AMP - Amplified Bible
MSG - The Message
NCV - New Century Version
GNT - Goodnews Translation

The material contained in this book is provided for informational purposes only. It is not intended to diagnose, provide medical advice, or take the place of medical advice and treatment from your personal physician.
The author in no way claims to be a medical professional. Readers are advised to consult qualified health professionals regarding mental, health, and personal issues.
Neither the publisher nor the author is responsible for any possible consequences for any person reading or following the information in this book.

Table of Content

A Boy ~ 6

A Father ~ 7

Age ~ 9

A Leader ~ 10

A Man ~ 12

A Mother ~ 13

Appreciation ~ 15

A Woman ~ 16

Beauty ~ 18

Celibacy ~ 19

Change ~ 21

Children ~ 22

Dating ~ 24

Days ~ 25

Death ~ 27

Depression ~ 29

Encouragement ~ 30

Faith ~ 32

Friendship ~ 33

God ~ 35

Growing up/Maturity ~ 36

High Achiever ~ 38

Husband ~ 39

Influences ~ 41

Inspiration ~ 42

Life ~ 44

Love ~ 45

Marriage ~ 47

Parent ~ 48

Patience ~ 50

Peace ~ 51

Press ~ 53

Relationship ~ 54

Self-love ~ 56

Spiritual Race ~ 57

Trust ~ 59

Wife ~ 60

Who's your Type ~ 62

Worry ~ 63

Introduction

In 2019, I wrote this Book of Inspirational Short Sayings & Quotes for enjoyment, encouragement, and reflection. For, life is a gift from God, and we should enjoy it every day and people love reading quotes. Especially, in the times we are living in right now. Nowadays, we find ourselves crying or praying more than we do laughing. Well, I know all about that and have had my fair share. Nevertheless, we cannot let life keep us down. I am extremely excited to present this book of short sayings and quotes to you. I pray that it blesses you the way that it has blessed me. Enjoy!

Acknowledgments

To My Lord and Savior Jesus Christ, I thank you for your wisdom, knowledge, and understanding of your word that you have poured into me. And thank you for your love and relationship. I will continue to press toward the mark of the high calling!

To my children, Jessica Koonce (decreased), Brittney Kornegay, Evonie Grant, DeJohn Kornegay, Shamyra Giddens, Tyriek, and Elijah Kornegay. And my daughter and sons-in-love thank you for your support and for allowing me to be the best version of myself. And to my twelve precious grandchildren whom I adore so much, thank you for loving Nannythe way that you all do. My drive and all that I do comes from all of you. "I am striving every day to be the best example of Christ I can be to you all!"

My mother MaryAnn Prince, father (deceased), siblings, family, and friends; thank you all so much for all your support, words of encouragement, and love. And a special thanks to Marsha Robinson, my sister in Christ, critic, and proofreader. To David Hawkins my brother in Christ, my printer, illustrator, and creator of my logo. Thank you for your prayers and our church service conversations! To your beautiful wife Kerise Hawkins thank you, are beautiful inside and out. David is blessed to have you! I am forever grateful to you!

Scripture:
"When I was a child, I spoke like a child, I thought like a child, I reasoned like a child. When I became a man, I gave up childish ways." (1 Corinthians 13:11 ESV)

A Boy

"Boys should always respect and love their mothers because it shows their worth!"

"Some boys run away from their responsibilities while others learn to man up!"

"Not all boys are a one woman's man, but they should be because their eyes are bigger than their pockets and integrity!"

"A mature guy doesn't want a lady with no goals, hopes, or dreams because that would be like going on a trip to nowhere!"

"A lady doesn't want a boy who invaded a man's body. She wants a guy who has embraced his manhood and knows who he is and where he's going!"

Scripture:
"See what great love the Father has lavished on us, that we should be called children of God! And that is what we are!"
(1 John 3:1 NIV)

A Father

"When the father loves, he loves hard and chases after whom he loves. So, be glad he has you in his thoughts!"
"God is a provider, protector, priest, and chief-in-command. And when he calls, answer because he's a keeper, healer, deliverer, and way maker!"
"Fathers come and go, but God said, "He will never leave you nor forsake you!"
"God will protect you from whom he doesn't want you to see or cross paths with!"
"God is the best father in the Universe! He never causes confusion or tells your secrets because he's faithful, and his love is unconditional!"
"A real and true father never abandons his kids! Just because he loses his position, his title never changes!"

Scripture:
"Even to your old age and gray hairs, I am he, I am he who will sustain you. I have made you and I will carry you; I will sustain you and I will rescue you."
(Isaiah 46:4 NIV)

Age

"Age is not fair because, without permission, your body starts behaving like a baby and an old man at the same time!" "Old age is not fair when bathroom trips require babywipes!" "The older you get, the more stubborn and set in your ways you become, making everybody's life miserable but not on purpose!"
"Age is like a thief because it steals your words right out your mouth causing your memory to lapse!" "Old age causes you to start fights with everyone who enters your home because you can't remember where you put things!" "Age ain't fair! Especially, when women who suffer from menopause start acting like their body temperature is bipolar!"

Scripture:
"Let us not become weary in doing good, for at the proper time we will reap a harvest if we do not give up."
(Galatians 6:9 NIV)

A leader

"Leaders never tell their staff's business. Followers do! Real leaders understand the importance of confidentiality under circumstances!"

"A leader should never deceive their workers because the very ones they despise could be the ones who rescue them out of trouble!"

"If a leader has problems with everyone they manage, is the problem the employees or the leader? As leaders, we must look at our reflection daily!"

"A good leader will establish a suitable and conducive culture for the business and his employees!"

"Leaders should be cautious of the seeds they plant within their business because what they sow, they will reap!"

"A good leader not only practices what he preaches. They make and follow their own rules and regulations!"

Scripture:
"Be watchful, stand firm in the faith, act like men, be strong. Let all that you do be done in love."
(1 Corinthians 16:13 ESV)

A Man

"When a man first meets a woman, he knows whether he wants to play or stay!"
"It's been said that a good man is hard to come across, but trust God to send the right one your way!"
"When a man hides his sexy behind his uniform, work flows as usual, and everyone gets to keep their job!"
"Before a man enters a woman's life, he should have himself together. So, they can love each other how they deserve to be loved!"
"A God-fearing man learns to do what pleases God more than what pleases himself because he understands that God will never fail him!"
"A man should never play with a woman's heart because she can respect him more if he considers her feelings!"

Scripture:
"Strength and honor are her clothing; she shall rejoice in time to come." (Proverbs 31:25 NKJV)

A Mother

"A mother's greatest joy is the birth of her child, and her worst nightmare is losing one!"
"A mother's worst pain is when she gives so much to her children and gets back so little!"
"It is possible for a mother to dislike who she birthed! Especially when she can't identify the child she raised!"
"Mother's Day comes once a year, but her job is never done. So, celebrate her every day!" "Childbirth can be gory but beautiful. Nevertheless, the pain was all worthwhile when a mother meets her baby for the first time!"
"A mother should always raise her children believing they are royalty because they were born to a king and queen!"

Scripture:
"Whatever you do, in word or in deed, do everything in the name of the Lord Jesus, giving thanks to God the Father through him."(Colossians 3:17 CSB)

Appreciation

"It's nice to let people know you appreciate them. So, speak life into them because they need to hear it!" "Learn to appreciate people for who they are because you don't know how long they'll be around!"
"We must learn to appreciate every gift God gives us because we are truly unworthy of them! But he finds it fit to bless us!"
"Be appreciative and show it by speaking volumes to those who bend over backward for you!"
"Appreciate the people God has placed in your life because your days are numbered!"
"Husbands and wives, always show that you love, care, respect, and appreciate each other because doing so, will keep the fire lit!"

Scripture:
"You made all the delicate, inner parts of my body and knit me together in my mother's womb. Thank you for making me so wonderfully complex! Your workmanship is marvelous- how well I know it." (Psalm 139:13-14 NLT)

A Woman

"When the right man enters a woman's life, she becomes overjoyed because she feels like she can breathe easy, be herself and conquer the world with him by her side!"
"Every woman likes to be protected because there's nothing like feeling safe in the arms of someone who loves her!"
"A woman can't make a man love her; he must want to! And what he won't do, another man will!"
"A real woman learns how to correct her mistakes when she finds herself at fault!"
"A strong woman learns that it's okay to be the weaker vessel. For, she trusts that her husband won't take advantage of her but will treat her like the queen she is!"
"A woman never has to question a faithful man's motives because love won't let him hide them!"

Scripture:
"For the Lord sees not as man sees; for man looks at the outward appearance, but the LORD looks at the heart."
(1 Samuel 16:7b AMP)

Beauty

"Your beauty is flawless because you're fearfully and wonderfully made! For, God stamped, sealed, and validated you!"
"It's been said, "that beauty is in the eyes of the beholder." Nowadays, people must look deeper because looks don't determine attitudes!"
"Some men want more than a pretty face. They want an intelligent woman who genuinely loves, respects, and cares for them because there's beauty in that!" "It's bad for a woman to have no home training, class, standards, morals, nor values and wanna meet their man's mother! She will be waiting for a long time!"
"It is important for every woman to feel and look beautiful! For her beauty affects her confidence, affects her beauty! So, compliment her!"
"The world is still a beautiful place even amid all the chaos! So, be the light and salt that adds favor!"

Scripture:
"Now for the matters you wrote about: "It is good for a man not to have sexual relations with a woman." But since sexual immorality is occurring, each man should have sexual relations with his own wife, and each woman with her own husband." (1 Corinthians 7:1-2 MSG)

Celibacy

"Celibacy isn't easy, but the only one you should want is your husband!"

"Choosing celibacy keeps you pure! So, value yourself enough not to let a stranger touch all over you like you're a raw piece of meat!"

"Celibacy is a choice! So, choose to wait for the right man to come along, sweep you off your feet, marry you, and eat your cooking too!"

"To live a celibate life, you must have a made-up mind and the right attitude!"

"Being celibate teaches you to stay committed to yourself and the right person, who will make you appreciate why you waited in the first place!"

"Celibacy is not for everyone because some people don't want to have self-control!"

Scripture:
"To everything there is a season, A time for every purpose under heaven." (Ecclesiastes 3:1 NKJV)

Change

"Words are just words until you put them into action because if you don't move, you are just talking!" "In life, you have to enforce new habits so they can push you into purpose!" "You are better than what you are settling for!" "If you're working hard to improve yourself, you should wait for what you deserve!"

"Only God can change a man, but even then, he has to want it!"

"There are some things we can't change, our parents, siblings, children, life, and death! So, we learn to live with them!"

Scripture:
"Children are a heritage from the LORD, offspring a reward from him. Like arrows in the hands of a warrior, are children born in one's youth." (Psalm 127:3-4 NIV)

Children

"Having children today is like a marriage. It's until death do you part!"
"God gives us children when we need them the most. Especially when we needed to get a grip!"
"Children can be such a blessing; they will teach you how to become selfless and discover yourself!"
"A child is a barren mother's pride and joy when she sees her miracle for the first time!"
"Children are gifts from God and your seeds that start new generations. So, raise them in the way that is pleasing to God! That he may say,
"Well done!"
"Children are such a joy and full of laughter!
Especially, when they start repeating things you've said at the wrong time!"

Scripture:
"Complete my joy being of the same mind, having the same love, being in full accord and of one mind. Do nothing from selfish ambition or conceit, but in humility count others more significant than yourselves."
(Philippians 2:2-3 ESV)

Dating

"Nowadays, dating requires an application and a fee!"
"The same way an employer interviews you for hire, you should interview your mate because a relationship is hard work!"
"If you're picky when you shop for clothes and shoes, you should be picky about who wants to date you!"
"Dating is like a woman shopping; time-consuming and picky!"
"Before you start dating, you be like, "I wanna cute guy," but cute goes out the window when his personality and attitude are ugly!"
"If dating leads you to marriage, consider these things respect, honor, loyalty, and never expect what you can't give!"

Scripture:
"Sunshine is sweet; it is good to see the light of day."
(Ecclesiastes 11:7 NCV)

Days

"Just because it's snowing outside doesn't mean the sun is not shining; God is the sun on a cloudy day!" "There's nothing like sunshine on a bright, cold winter day that shines and warms you up!"

"Cloudy days don't stop a show, even when you can't see sunshine. Know it's there because you woke up to a beautiful day!"

"It's morning, another day you have been granted to get what you left undone. Yet, be grateful you're still on the clock!"

"The love of your life can cause the sun to shine on your darkest day!"

"No matter what season it is in your life, still declare it's sunny outside!"

Scripture:
"Jesus say to them, my time has not yet come, but your time is always here." (John 7:6 ESV)

Death

"One never knows when a death angel will knock on their door! So, live your best life every day, free from worries!"
"Death is not the end of life; it's the beginning because it is in that moment that all earthly cares disappear!"
"Count your blessings because somebody's alarm rang, but they didn't wake up!"
"Sometimes, death can come expectedly, and when it does, we're still not ready for it!"
"Celebrate your loved ones when they die because they are free from this world!"
"The only things death leaves you with are an obituary, soggy tissues, memories, and overdue bills!"

Scripture:
"Answer me quickly, Lord; my spirit fails. Do not hide your face from me, or I will be like those who go down to the pit." (Psalm 143:7-9 NIV)

Depression

"Fear and faith goes hand and hand because fear makes you fight while faith gives you the courage to push back!"
"When life throws curve balls, throw them back because It's your downfalls that teaches life's greatest lessons to stand!"
"Never let the cares of life weigh you down! When God is constantly telling you to cast care upon him.
For he cares for you!" "Depression is a thief of a man's joy because the
enemy wants to rob you of your gifts, but you must fight to live!"
"Depression is a spirit that depresses people, but anything pressed down must spring forward!"
"The enemy wants you to stay depressed because he knows you're valuable to God!"

Scripture:
"Therefore encourage one another and build one another up, just as you are doing." (1 Thessalonians 5:11 ESV)

Encouragement

"God's daily remedy is, "a scripture a day will keep the devil away!"
"To know to do better and choose not to, leads to failure!"
"Live your best life because nobody's blocking you but you!"
"Be your own inspirational speaker! For God already breathed in you!"
"There's no door too heavy for God to open! For God's promises are yea and amen!"
"God doesn't give do-overs; he gives makeovers!"

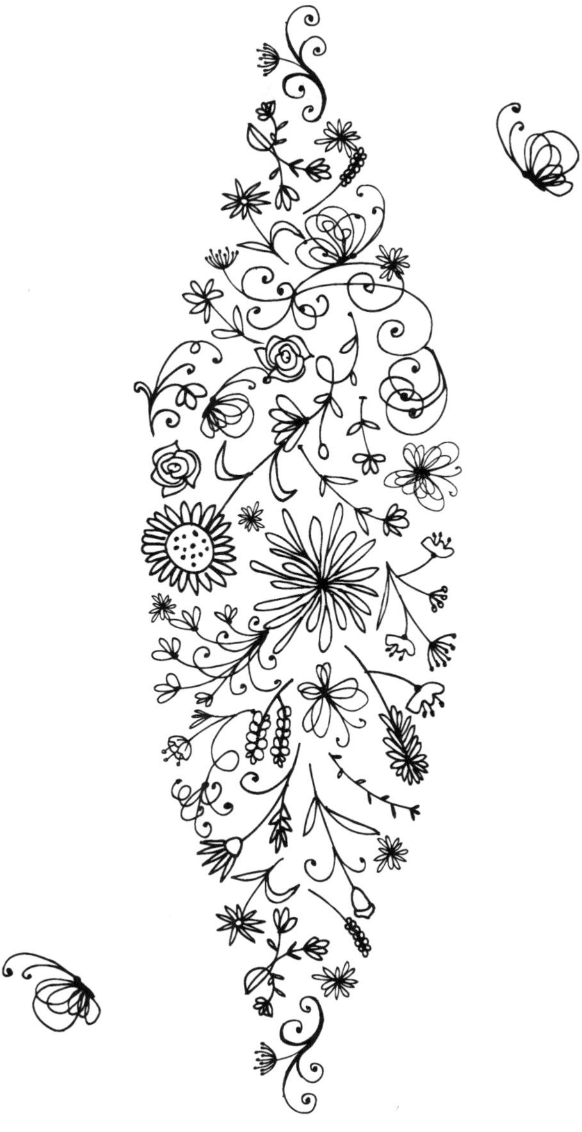

Scripture:
"Now faith is the substance of things hoped for, the evidence of things not seen." (Hebrew 11:1 KJV)

Faith

"Faith requires trust and courage, requires faith. Without them, you will accomplish nothing!" "Stay faithful to what you've been called to, and watch God bless you!"
"Nothing happens by surprise, but everything happens for a reason. For there is nothing that God does not know!"
"When you believe God for something, you must have faith and believe his report!"
"A man who trusts God for the woman he gave him knows their life won't be perfect but blessed!"
"Take a leap and show God your faith!"

Scripture:
"Above all, keep loving one another earnestly, since love covers a multitude of sins. Show hospitality to one another without grumbling. As each has received a gift, use it to serve one another, as good stewards of God's varied grace."
(1 Peter 4:8-10 ESV)

Friendship

"Friendships should be built on loyalty and love. And if you can't be loyal, why should you be called friend!"
"I've been told that good friends are hard to find. So, hold dear to them and show them that you're grateful to be a part of their life!"
"Friendship is important because it can be the foundation of a great relationship and true love!" "Friendship carries so much weight because you don't get many. People tend to put associates and friends in the same category, but they cannot compare!"
"Friends go the extra mile to love you wholeheartedly, they want to see you happy, and always have your back, but associates come and go, just like the wind!"
"Friends who build a healthy relationship are off to a great start!"

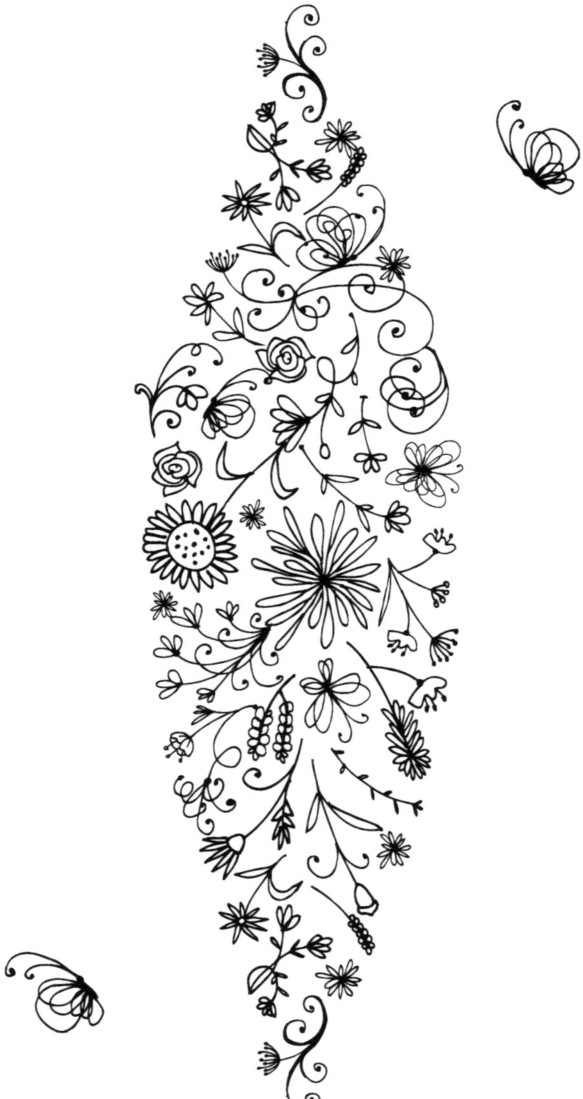

Scripture:
"So do not fear, for I am with you; do not be dismayed, for I am your God. I will strengthen you and help you; I will uphold you with my righteous right hand."
(Isaiah 41:10 NIV)

God

"It is so wonderful to know that God covers and keeps us. He loves us despite our flaws!"
"A relationship with God must become our norm because, without him, we are nothing!"
"God didn't create love for you to fear it; he created it so you would always run to it!"
"Some people come into your life to make you. While others come to break you. Yet, God prepares you for both!"
"God has given us gifts, and we've mishandled what He has given us! And, he still gives us a second chance!
"When you pray for things, learn to ask God to prepare you for what you're asking him for!"

Scripture:
"Let those of us who are mature think this way, and if in anything you think otherwise, God will reveal that also to you!"
(Philippians 3:15 ESV)

Growing up / Maturity

"Maturity is not just what you say. It's what you do!"
"Maturity teaches responsibility, respect, and how to have a genuine love for self and others!"
"If you find yourself doing the same things you did as a teenager, change your mindset!"
"Just because you've reached a mature age doesn't mean you've grown! "For age doesn't define maturity!"
"Some say, "they're grown but still live at home and don't want to pay bills!"
"Some people had to grow up fast because they stepped into arenas, they had no business in!"

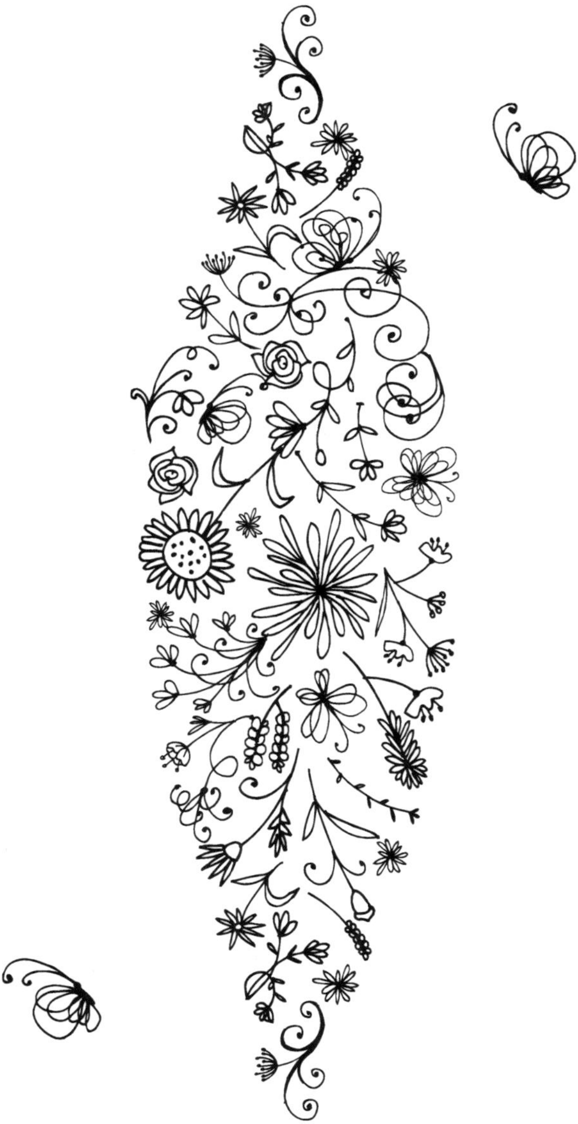

Scripture:
"Trust in the LORD with all your heart and lean not on your own understanding; in all your ways submit to him, and he will make your paths straight."
(Proverbs 3:5-6 NIV)

High Achiever

"High achievers don't go down without a fight!" "They believe their dreams have no limitations!" "High achievers never take no for an answer! They press consistently towards their goals and believe that when one door closes, a better door opens!"

"Someone who believes their gift will make room for them will work for free until it becomes a reality!" "Someone who wants anything bad enough, work hard until they see it come to pass!"

"High achievers learn to pray much, have faith and trust in God!"

Scripture:
"Husbands, love your wives, even as Christ also loved the church, and gave himself for it; So, ought men to love their wives as their bodies. He that loveth his wife loveth himself."(Ephesians 5:25, 28 NKJV)

Husband

"Husband, it's normal for you to think about the possibilities of your heart getting broken, but perfect love casts out fear. In other words, "you won't regret it if it's right!"

"A husband is the one whom God calls, the head of household, protector, provider, and the one he commands to love his wife and be on one accord with her!"

"Husbands, love your wives! She is your friend, partner, and help mate, not your maid but your Queen! So, treat her with respect!"

"Marriage is a huge responsibility, and now that you're married, it doesn't mean you're done working. It just means you have two jobs!"

"It seems like it took you a lifetime to meet your soulmate. Now, that you have her treat her like a queen; and she will bring you great joy!"

"A good husband will never leave his wife uncovered for another man to come along and sweep her off her feet because he keeps her satisfied!"

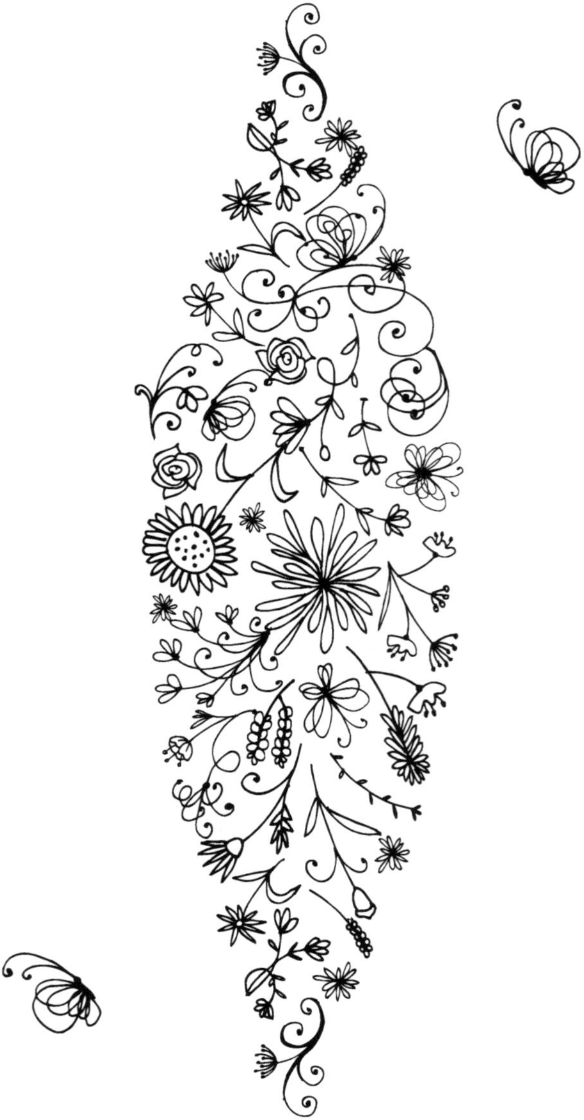

Scripture:
"Iron sharpens iron, and one man sharpens another."
(Proverbs 27:17 ESV)

Influences

"If you see me with people that look like gangsters, don't be alarmed! They're a host of angels who came to put those demons in their place!"

"If you know you are the solution, don't allow anyone to cause you to become the problem!" "It's better to be a leader, not a follower, and if you're going to be a follower, be a follower of good leadership!"

"As parents, it is important to be cognitive of the influences you bring around your children because the consequences will be on you!"

"The power of influence is a strong spirit! Especially, when people have no sense of who they are!"

"You must be careful of the company you keep because everyone doesn't have your best interest at heart!

Scripture:
"But he said to me, "My grace is sufficient for you, for my power is made perfect in weakness. "Therefore I will boast all the more gladly of my weaknesses, so that the power of Christ may rest upon me." (2 Corinthians 12:9 ESV)

Inspiration

"Goals, dreams, aspirations, and visions all share the same purpose. They inspire you to move forward!"
"Love your life because someone didn't make it off the delivery table!"
"When people speak negativity over your life, remind them that they're cursing themselves!" *"Moving up ceremonies inspire those who accomplish their goals to be inspired and continue on their journey. In the hope that their spectators will follow!"*
"If you want to be inspired, hang around inspirational people who are where you are going!" *"If you want to be inspired, watch toddlers. They are not afraid of anything!"*

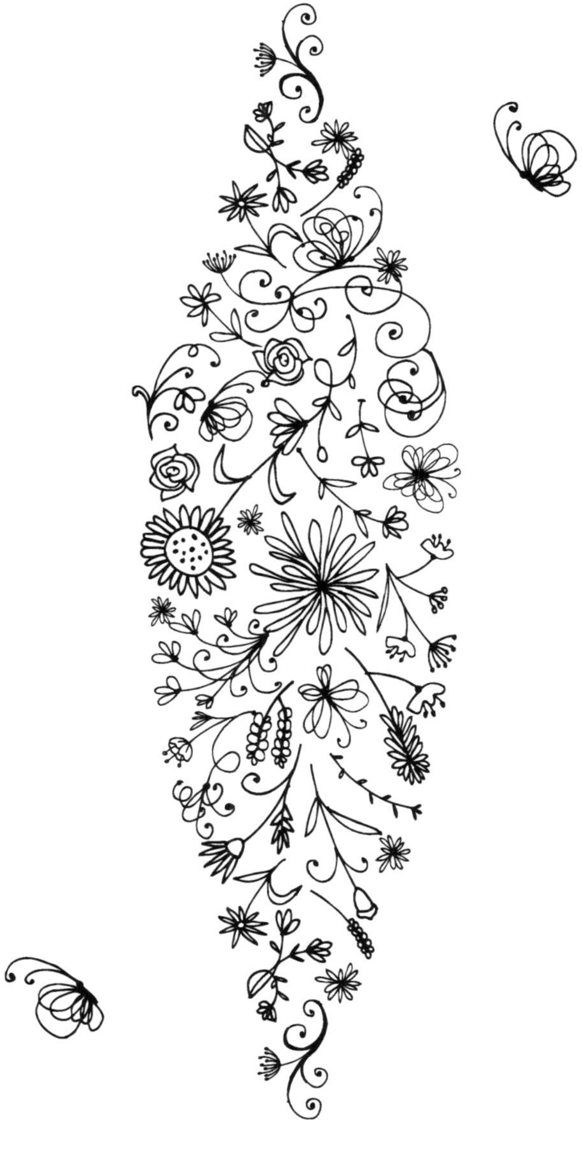

Scripture:
"The LORD will keep you from all evil; he will keep your life. The LORD will keep your going out and your coming in from this time forth and forevermore."
(Psalm 121:7-8 ESV)

Life

"Back in the days, grandparents took their grands to church, but they didn't realize they gave them the greatest gift in the world, Jesus Christ!"
"Every day, you're blessed because God blew his breath into you and woke you up this morning!" "Life is what you make of it because you have the power to speak life or death to every situation!"
"Life is like a maze, many doors to go through but only one door out!"
"Life can become very difficult when you allow people to dictate who we are!"
"It's been said, "that life is what you make it! So, practice living stress-free, believing that whatever you desire, you shall have!"

Scripture:
"Love never gives up. Love cares more for others than for self. Love doesn't want what it doesn't have. Love doesn't strut, Doesn't have a swelled head, Doesn't force itself on other, isn't always "me first," Doesn't fly off the handle, Doesn't keep score of the sins of others."
(1 Corinthians 13:4-5 MSG)

Love

"True love doesn't come so easy, but when it shows up, don't miss it wondering whether it's true or not!" "Love doesn't fail people. People fail love because it speaks without question!"

"You wanna know love, seek after God! For he created it, His actions show it, His language talks it, His feet walk it, and his breath breathes it!"

"The funny thing about love is, when it loves, regardless of flaws. For, love is a matter of the heart!"

"Love can last a lifetime if you're willing to give it, forever and a day!"

"Love can be like a spider web. Once you get caught in it, it's hard to get out of!"

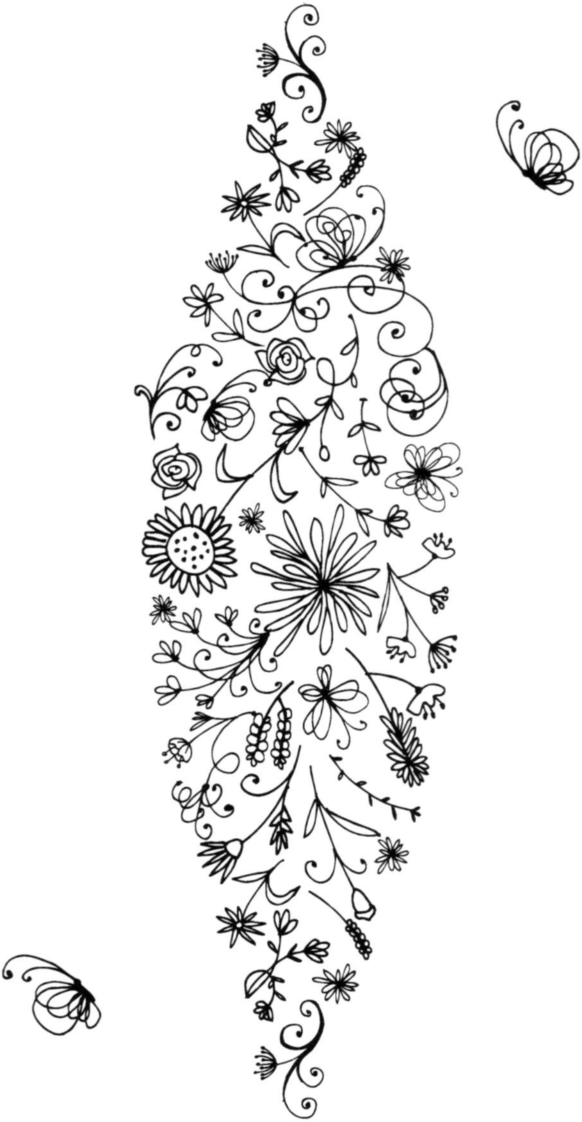

Scripture:
"Be completely humble and gentle; be patient, bearing with one another in love. Make every effort to keep the unity of the Spirit through the bond of peace."
(Ephesians 4:2-3 NIV)

Marriage

"Marriage is a special bond of commitment made between two people; God bless this union until death do them part!"
"Marriage is pleasing to the Lord! So, do right that he may smile upon it!"
"Marriage is a partnership between two people who agreed to walk, talk and do almost everything together!"
"What an honor for you to love her past her faults. You saw her needs and realized you would meet her acquaintance in marriage!"
"In marriage, you give up your singleness to become as one, not to have security or to still play the field!" *"Some marry for love, others for benefits. Yet, marriage is give and receive, not give, and take. Both of you should have full hands!"*

Scripture:
"Children, obey your parents in the Lord, for this is right."
(Ephesians 6:1 ESV)

Parent

"The differences between yesterdays and today's parents are that they ask the kids what they want to do. "While yesterday's parents gave them no choice!"
"Some women are determined not to be like their mothers. Yet not everything she did was wrong! Look how you turned out!"
"Your parents are your parents because only their DNA could create you! And those are the FACTS! So, thank God for your parents!" "Parents, children should not be asked to make
decisions you should make yourself! That's why God gave you the title; parent!"
"One of a parent's greatest superpowers is selective hearings, so use it wisely when your children act out!"¶
"A parent's job is to raise, train and steer their children towards their goals, not carry them all the way to the finish line!"

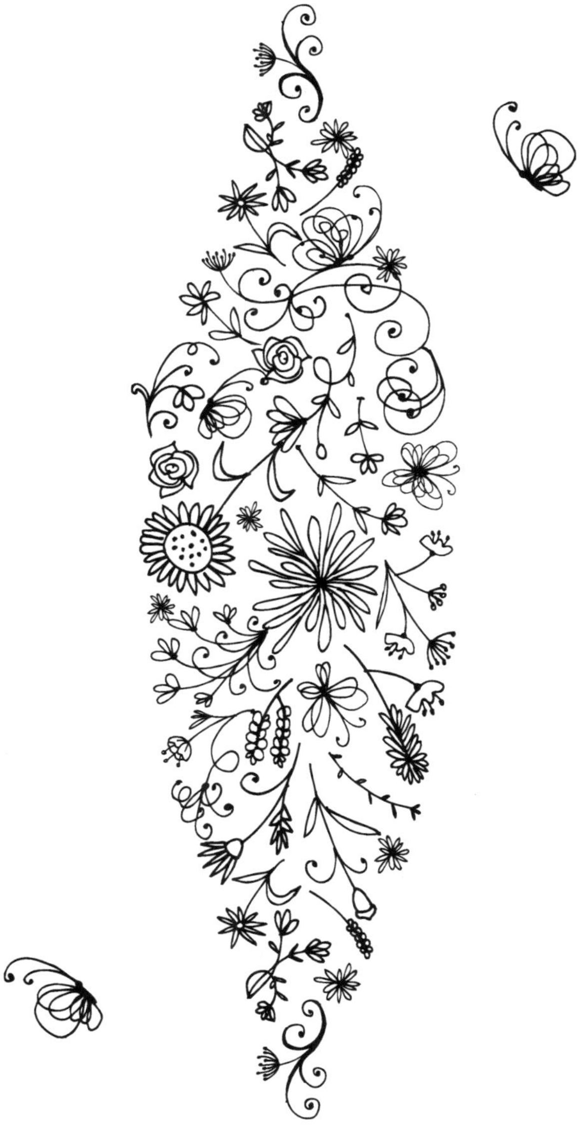

Scripture:
"The LORD is good to everyone who trusts in him, so it is best for us to wait in patience- to wait for him to save us- And it is best to learn this patience in our youth." (Lamentations 3:25-27 GNT)

Patience

"In your patience, allow yourself to be made because patience causes growth and maturity!"

"As a parent, if you don't learn anything else, you must learn patience because if you don't, you will lose yourself and your children!"

"Some people have been waiting for love a long time, but we can't rush God because some surgeries take longer than others!"

"When love shows up in your life, you will know it. So, take your time and keep God in the center of it!" *"No one wants to be alone, nor do they want to be with the wrong person! So, wait for the one that God has approved for you!"*

"So many people are always in a rush to go somewhere, but proper time management gets you there on time!"

Scripture:
"Let him turn away from evil and do good; Let him seek peace and pursue it." (1 Peter 3:11 NKJV)

Peace

"It's not that we can't live in peace and harmony because we can, but some just love chaos and drama more!"

"Today, if you want peace, you must find it within yourself and take it wherever you go!"

"The world is changing so much with hardly any place to run or hide for peace; we must carry this in our hearts. So, wherever we go, it will be there!" *"When you are a peacemaker, you should always want to see people getting along because we already have enough angry people!"*

"Some people in this world want peace but don't want the Prince, who can give them peace! For Jesus is the Prince of Peace!"

"There is true peace and rest in the Lord's arms!"

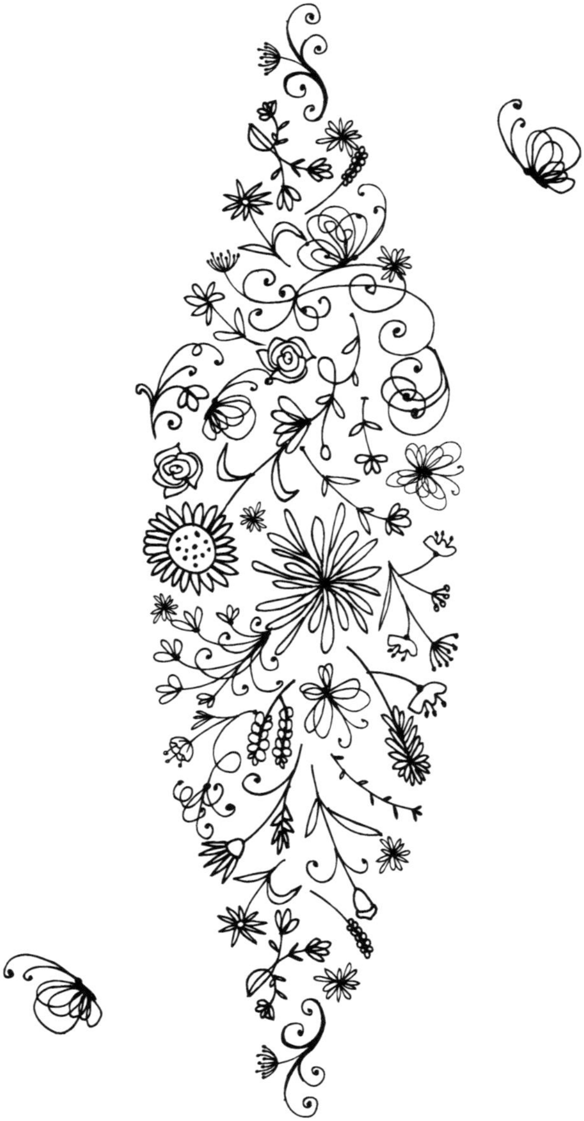

Scripture:
"I press toward the goal for the prize of the upward call of God in Christ Jesus." (Philippians 3:14 NKJV)

Press

"If birds of a feather flock together! Soar with the eagles!"
"Anything you want in life, you have to work hard for it because when you work hard, you appreciate it more!"
"When you are enthusiastic about something you want, you'll work on it day and night!"
"Life can be overwhelming, but no matter what stumbling blocks get in your way, leap towards your goals!"
"There's no goal too far that you can't reach. The first rule is never to give up!"
"Some people were born with a silver spoon in their mouth, and still, nothing is easy! Life happens to everyone!"

Scripture:
"Above all, love each other deeply because love covers a multitude of sins." (1 Peter 4:8 NIV)

Relationship

"If you really love yourself, you would take the time to get yourself together before you commit to loving someone else!"
"True love can last a lifetime if you want it, but it will take hard work and effort because nothing happens overnight!"
"When you find the love of your life, don't let them go because love doesn't come by often! True love is hard to find but possible. So, thanks for calling out the search party!"
"Relationships are built on how you treat, love, respect, and care for an individual!"
"Every relationship gains strength through trust! For trust grows good health and prosperity!"
"People can be so fickle, one day, they're up, and the next day, they're down! But God is the same yesterday, today, and forever!"

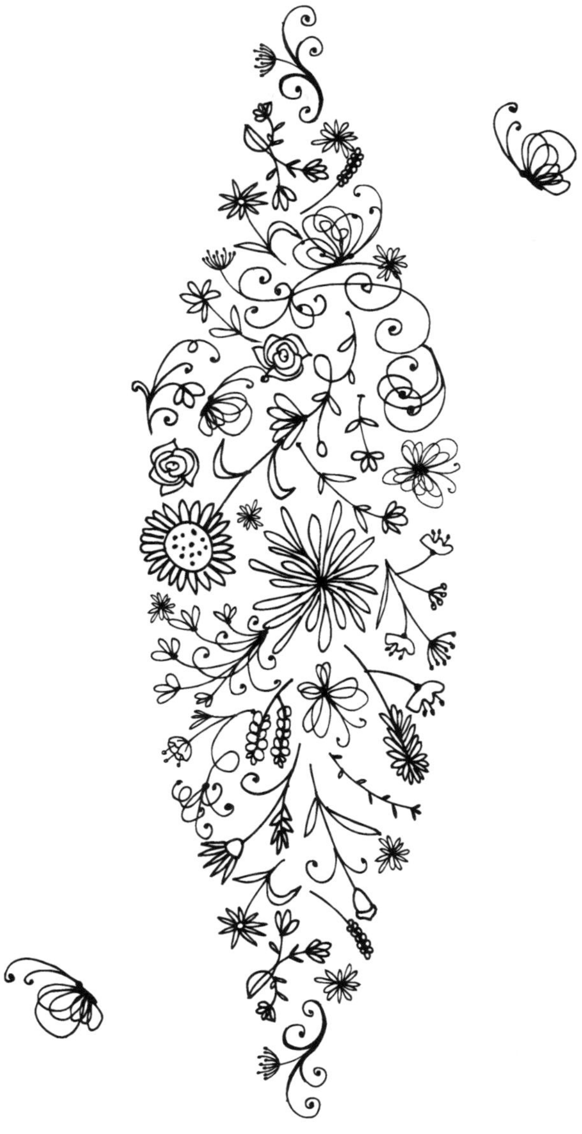

Scripture:
"I can do all things through Christ who strengthens me."
(Philippians 4:13 NKJV)

Self-Love

"Boys want mamas while men want wives. So, which one do you prefer?"
"So many people walk around with such a chip on their shoulder as if they don't need love, but they do!"
"If you don't enjoy being in your own company, why should anyone else? Learn how to enjoy your own presence so others can too!"
"When you know who you are, you don't have to explain yourself because it shows in how you carry yourself!"
"Self-love is a given, but if you have never been taught to love yourself, how can or do you?"
"Don't be eye candy, be soul food!"
"Love yourself enough for all to see so when someone comes into your life, they will know how to love you!"

Scripture:
"I press on toward the goal for the prize of the upward call of God in Christ Jesus." (Philippians 3:14 ESV)

Spiritual Race

"Some of us were called "church-girl," growing up, and now that you're grown, they call us, "a woman of God," cause you stayed in the race!"

"Your prayer life should be as real as spiritual warfare because we need to be covered every day!" "When you are on a spiritual journey, you're going to run into challenges, but what makes it easier is your obedience to God!"

"Spiritual warfare is all around us, and it only seems like the bad are winning but we are on a team that doesn't lose battles!"

"Two wars are happening: the one inside and around you. And you need to pay attention to both!" "Some people have been running all their life when all they had to do was call on Jesus!"

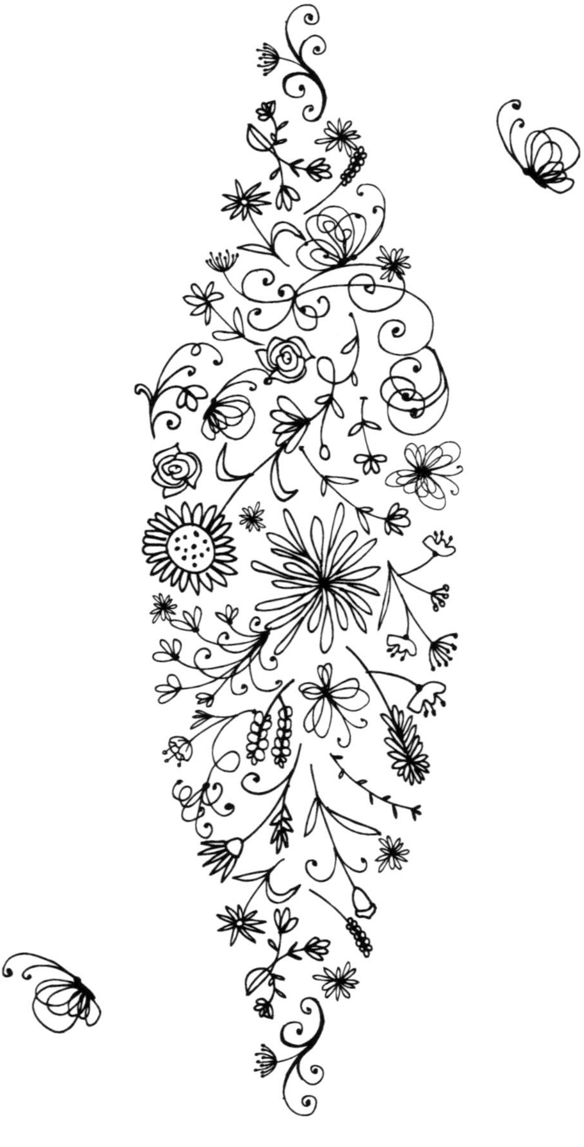

Scripture:
"Trust in the Lord with all your heart, and do not lean on your own understanding. In all your ways acknowledge him, and he will make straight your paths."
(Proverbs 3:5-6 ESV)

Trust

"God makes life worth living because if it's not your time, trust him to wake you up every morning!"
"Once you know that you've done your best in a relationship, you can walk away with your head held high and still have love in your heart!"
"When someone trusts you enough to put their heart in your hands, don't break it!"
"An answer is better than no answer. For, there are only two responses you can give; yes, or no!" "When you can't trust yourself, trust God!"
"Stop doing what's comfortable, believe God, and go through the open door! But once he gives it to you, "handle it with care!"

Scripture:
"Then the LORD God made a woman from the rib he had taken out of the man, and he brought her to the man." (Genesis 2:22 NIV)

Wife

"The most loyal thing is a celibate woman who has chosen to wait on her husband!"

"Every woman wants a husband who will supply all her needs! So, she waits on God because only he can fill that order!"

"A wife is a gift from God. Yet, some men still don't understand the blessings that come with being a husband!"

"A woman who values her husband works hard to prepare herself before he arrives. And if she's smart, she continues to work hard to keep him!"

"A wife's submission to her husband honors her God! How she treats, honors, and respects God is the same way He expects her to behave toward her husband!"

"A wife-in-training learns to pray for her husband before she meets him because she already loves him!"

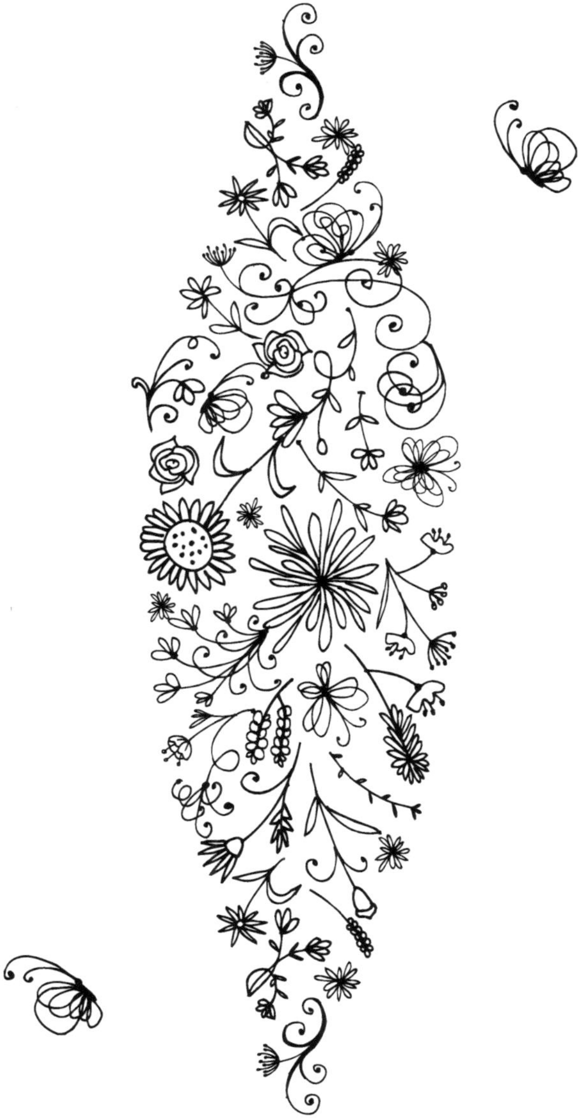

Scripture
*"The Lord God said, it is not good for the man to be alone.
I will make a helper suitable for him."
(Genesis 2:18 NIV)*

Who's Your Type

"Who's your type, is the one you least expect. And everything you could ever want and need, but you keep looking past him!"

*"Ladies, stop looking for a man and let him find you.
Just pay attention to his qualities, not his imperfections!"*

"When a woman knows who she truly is, any man can't approach her, not because she thinks she's better than him but because she knows her worth!"

"It's been said, "that you meet no one but yourself!" So, knowing what you want teaches you what you ought to give!"

"Some men want a woman with class! While others want a quick fix, but some quick fixes aren't reversible!"

"A woman should raise her son to be the type of man she, herself, would want to marry! Because what's good for her should be good for someone else's daughter!"

Scripture:
"Can any one of you by worrying add a single hour to your life? And why do you worry about clothes? See how the flowers of the field grow. They do not labor or spin." (Matthew 6:27-28 NIV)

Worry

"Try not to worry about anything. Just give your worries to God because he already has the solution!"
"I was taught that there are different kinds of worries! Nevertheless, they all can lead to sickness!"
"Worrying is a sin because most people worry about what they can't change and don't have enough faith to believe in the one who can change it!"
"Worrying causes obstacles that hinder our blessings, so unlock the door by trusting God's word!
"Worry is like kryptonite because it weakens a man's ability to have faith!"

Thank You for Reading

The Book of Inspirational Short Sayings & Quotes

By Audrey J. Kornegay

Your Thoughts Here...

Your Thoughts Here...

Your Thoughts Here...

Your Thoughts Here...

Made in the USA
Columbia, SC
23 December 2024